Publisher's Note

This publication is designed to provide accurate and authoritative information in regard to the subject matter covered. It is sold with the understanding that the publisher is not engaged in rendering psychological, financial, legal, or other professional services. If expert assistance or counseling is needed, the services of a competent professional should be sought.

Distributed in Canada by Raincoast Books

Copyright © 2016 by
Laurie Grossman & Angelina Alvarez
New Harbinger Publications, Inc.
5674 Shattuck Avenue
Oakland, CA 94609
www.newharbinger.com

Library of Congress Cataloging-in-Publication Data on file

Printed in Canada

18   17

10   9   8   7   6

Master of Mindfulness:

How to Be Your Own Superhero in Times of Stress

of Stress

Kudos to the children in Mr. Musumeci's fifth grade class for writing this book for their peers. It is obvious from both the pictures and the text that mindfulness has been an important part of their learning to navigate through difficult times by befriending their own minds and recognizing new ways to deal with the hard stuff differently. What a useful classroom strategy to catalyze real learning by learning first how to deal with intrusive thoughts and emotions and with outer circumstances at home and at school more creatively and wholesomely. Bravo to these real heroes — never mind the super.

Jon Kabat-Zinn
Founder of Mindfulness-Based Stress Reduction (MBSR) and the Center for Mindfulness in Medicine, Health Care and Society
Professor of Medicine Emeritus
University of Massachusetts Medical School

What do you do when that happens?

You should try mindfulness!

We are fifth graders from Reach Academy in East Oakland, California. Miss Laurie taught us mindfulness in school but we use it in class, on the yard, where we live, and everywhere. Lots of us have taught our families and friends how to do it. We wrote this book so you could learn about mindfulness and have a better life, and live longer, and help each other. See students' names on page 63

We will show you how we have used mindfulness, and we'll teach you how to do it and how to find your own Master of Mindfulness. We recorded our voices so you could listen to us lead you in practices. You can go to http://www.newharbinger.com/34640 to download the recordings. If you want to listen to your own voice or to someone whose voice you like, feel free to record the mindfulness scripts at the end of this book.

What is mindfulness anyway?

Mindfulness is a precious thing. It means paying attention to your feelings, to how your friends and family are feeling, to the things you are learning about in school, to your actions and to playing sports. Mindfulness is really about paying attention to everything right now or as it happens, noticing it but not making a judgment about it.

Mindfulness can help you calm down and deal with difficult things. Mindfulness can also help you pay attention to the world, like hearing beautiful birds sing, really looking at colorful butterflies fluttering their wings, or noticing clouds when they move. It can even help you avoid distractions so you can concentrate better.

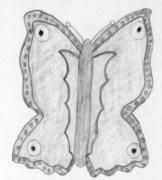

So, how do you know when you need mindfulness?

You'll know because you get mad and your fists ball up, your face might turn red (it doesn't matter what color you are), you might want to fight someone, or to throw something, or leave where you are.

or

You feel sad and your heart feels like it's broken and you want to stay at home.

or

You are embarrassed because your teacher calls on you when you aren't paying attention.

or

When you're taking a test, and your brain feels tight and you can't figure out the answer.

or

When people are mean to you and you might do something that gets you in trouble.

or

When the birds are chirping but you can't hear them because your thoughts are too busy.

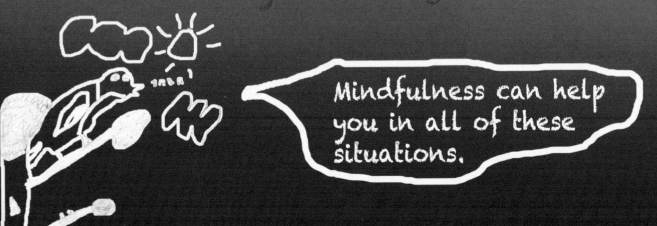

Mindfulness can help you in all of these situations.

5

WHEN THESE THINGS HAPPEN, YOU CAN HELP YOURSELF. JUST USE THE SHARKFIN AS YOUR SIGNAL TO CALL UP YOUR SUPERHERO.

One way to remember you need mindfulness is to call on your Sharkfin. To do the Sharkfin, you put the side of your hand on top of your head and then you move it down your face, in front of your nose, and say shhhh and close your eyes as your hand moves down. If you are sitting down, you do the 5 S's while you move your hand: Sit up straight, sit still, sit silently, soft breathing, shut eyes. If you are standing you do the same but you are standing straight, still, silently, using soft breathing and shut eyes while you move your hand down your face.

I used mindfulness when I got hit in the face with a soccer ball. Instead of getting mad at the person who kicked the ball and leaving the game, I took a few deep breaths

and realized I was scared but I was okay.
I kept playing.

Ouch!

Ouch!

7

When I got mad at myself for changing a password, and my computer wouldn't do what I wanted it to do so I couldn't play video games, I used mindfulness. This time I didn't holler, kick stuff and blame my sister. Instead I called my cousin and asked him what to do.

When my parents started fighting I went to my room and did mindfulness and it made me feel less nervous.

I used mindfulness when I felt jealous because my cousin got what I wanted. Instead of getting mad at him, I realized that we don't always get the same stuff.

NEW SHOES!

I used mindfulness when I couldn't play in my basketball game because I was late. Even though I took some breaths, I was still disappointed, but I also started cheering on my team. I stayed calm and recognized that I need to be more responsible.

When someone cut in front of me in line at the cafeteria, I used mindfulness to settle myself down and just let it be. Before I would get mad, push back, or hit someone. Sometimes we'd end up fighting and get in trouble. It's not worth it. It's easier to take a few breaths and calm down.

When I was having a good day, I taught my friend mindfulness.

Uso mindfulness para cuando estoy triste porque extraño a mi mama que está en México. Entonces empiezo a llorar and me acuerdo de ella, después me dice mi tía que no me ponga triste que la voy a ver muy pronto y respiro y uso mindful breathing entonces me siento mejor y me pongo feliz y mi tía también.

Si su madre está en México y no tiene una persona con quién hablar y si se siente sólo puede hacer mindfulness.

mindfulness / will help

I use mindfulness when I am sad because I miss my mom who is in Mexico. Then I start to cry because I think of her. Afterwards, my aunt tells me not to be sad because I am going to see her very soon. I use mindful breathing, then I feel better, and I get happy. My aunt does, too.

If your mom is in Mexico and you don't have anyone to talk to and you feel lonely, you can do mindfulness.

When a little fourth grader didn't say excuse me, I was about to say something, but instead I decided to just take a few breaths.

When we do mindfulness, it actually changes our brains and helps us make wise choices. Brain scientists are really interested in mindfulness and they are doing a lot of research and finding out that mindfulness is great for our brains. That's why it can make us feel better when times are hard,

like...

When my grandma was late picking
me up and I was worried, I
took some breaths. I talked to
my friends, stayed on the
bench and did my homework
while I waited for her.
When she got there I was calmer
and I asked her how her day
was instead of getting upset.

I used mindfulness when I got bullied by some girls and when my brother made fun of me.

IF SOMEONE BULLIES ME, I LEARNED THAT IT'S USUALLY BECAUSE THEY FEEL BAD ABOUT SOMETHING, SO THEY TRY AND TAKE IT OUT ON ME. MY SUPERHERO HELPS ME IN TIMES LIKE THESE! I HAVE AN IMAGINARY SHIELD THAT I PUT ON EVERY MORNING. IF SOMEONE IS BEING MEAN, MY SHARKFIN REMINDS MY SUPERHERO TO ACTIVATE MY SHIELD & WITH A FEW BREATHS THE MEAN STUFF CAN'T GET INTO MY HEART. THE GOOD STUFF CAN GET IN BUT MEAN JOKES AND COMMENTS CAN'T.

You can use mindfulness when someone tries to get you to do something you don't want to do, or asks you to go where you are not supposed to go, or does something that could get you in trouble.

I used mindfulness when my cousin left for Oklahoma and I was really sad. It helped me feel a little better. Instead of crying in my bed for days, I started thinking of how we could video chat and write letters to each other.

I was using mindfulness because I had a history project that stressed me out a lot. It helped me be less frustrated because I was able to focus on my work and do it little by little. Taking breaths helps me not procrastinate.

HOW DOES THIS ALL WORK?

Usually when you practice mindfulness it makes you feel calm and relaxed. The reason for this is that you are connecting four different parts of your brain: your prefrontal cortex, your limbic system which includes the hippocampus and the amygdala, and the brain stem. Brain cells are called neurons and there are almost 100 billion of them in our heads! When the neurons from the four parts of the brain touch each other we feel good; it's easier to concentrate, be kind, and make good decisions. To achieve this connection, you have to be aware of what is happening. For example, when you are practicing breathing, you know you are breathing, when you are angry, you recognize you're angry, when you are happy you know you are happy.

Amygdala

Hippocampus

Pre Frontal Cortex

Brain stem

Our brains are amazing but sometimes the way they work can get us in trouble. In order to keep us safe, brains look out for danger. The brain can't tell the difference between real danger and a small argument, or a broken toy. When the brain thinks we are in danger the amygdala gets activated, the hormones cortisol and adrenaline get released, and that's when we fight, flight, or freeze. We all know what fighting means. Flight means we run away and freeze means we can't do anything.

If we are in real danger, running away or fighting might be a good thing. However, when we have an argument with a friend, or we're yelled at by the teacher, we don't need to run or fight. If we're not really paying attention to how we are feeling, we are reacting instead of responding.

We actually "flip our lids" and the result is a variety of bad choices. It's so much easier and more fun to be mindful.

We can take some breaths. When we do that, the amygdala calms down, the three brain parts connect, and instead of screaming, hitting, throwing things, or running away, we can make a wise choice and the situation will turn out better.

When you are scared because someone you love is acting really mad, it's good to do mindfulness.

When you are really excited because it's your birthday, you can use mindfulness to calm down instead of using your excited energy to be disruptive and annoying.

I used mindfulness when I had to do chores I didn't want to do. Before knowing how to do mindfulness, I wouldn't do my chores and they would pile up. Now I do mindfulness and the chores aren't so bad. They get done quicker and sometimes I even do more than I thought I would.

Teachers should do a little mindfulness when the kids
don't pay attention and they feel frustrated.
Otherwise they will yell and lose control. Mindfulness
can help them be calmer.

Now, we are going to teach you how to do mindfulness so you can be your own superhero. If you practice mindfulness every day, then your superhero will be there, ready for you, when you are having strong feelings. You can even teach mindfulness to other people after you learn how to do it. We are going to teach you how to do mindful breathing, mindful noticing of your feelings, a body scan, mindful eating, mindful walking, and mindful being with each other.

To do mindfulness, you should find as quiet a place as you can. Then you sit down on a chair or on a bed. Put your feet flat so they are grounded on the floor. Then you do the Sharkfin.

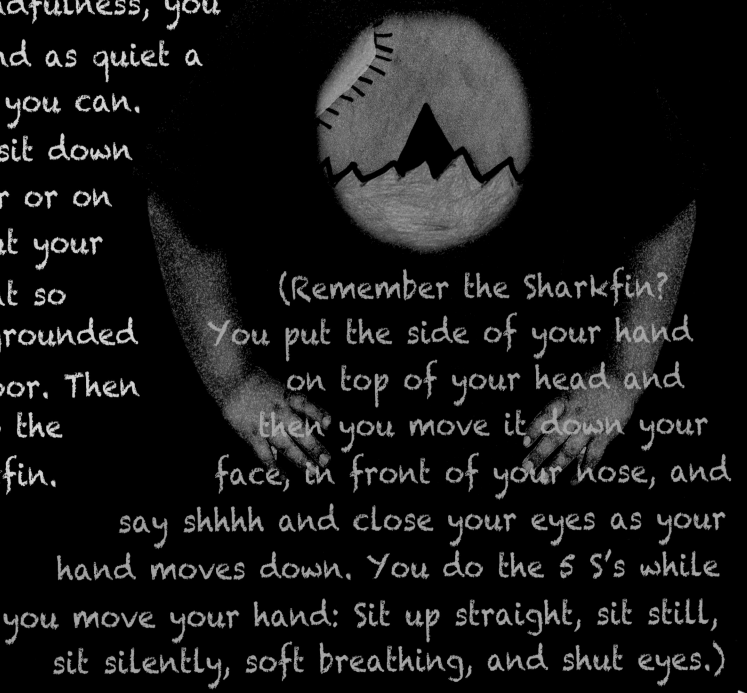

(Remember the Sharkfin? You put the side of your hand on top of your head and then you move it down your face, in front of your nose, and say shhhh and close your eyes as your hand moves down. You do the 5 S's while you move your hand: Sit up straight, sit still, sit silently, soft breathing, and shut eyes.)

Start mindful breathing by taking three deep breaths. You might feel your breath in and out of your nose, in your chest or in your stomach. Now, breathe normally and pay attention to your breath as it goes in and out of your body. You may feel your lungs filling up with air and feeling like everything is getting cleaned. Soon you may notice lots of thoughts. When is recess? What am I going to eat? Am I going to be first in line?

You may feel like your head is spinning. Suddenly you will realize you are thinking and that you aren't focusing on your breath. So then you just bring your attention back to your breath. (Never get mad at yourself for this.) You can do mindful breathing for one minute, or two, or three or as many as you want.

Sometimes things happen in life that are hard and you can't stop thinking about them. For example, if you have a fight with a friend or a family member, you can't get rid of the bad feelings that go along with that memory. To help you get rid of the feeling you have to notice it, which is what mindfulness does. When you have the feeling, say to yourself, "There's that feeling, thanks for noticing _____(your name)," and pat yourself on the shoulder at the same time. Doing this can help you recognize your feelings and that can help you stop thinking about bad memories which can help you succeed in school, in sports, or in having good times at home.

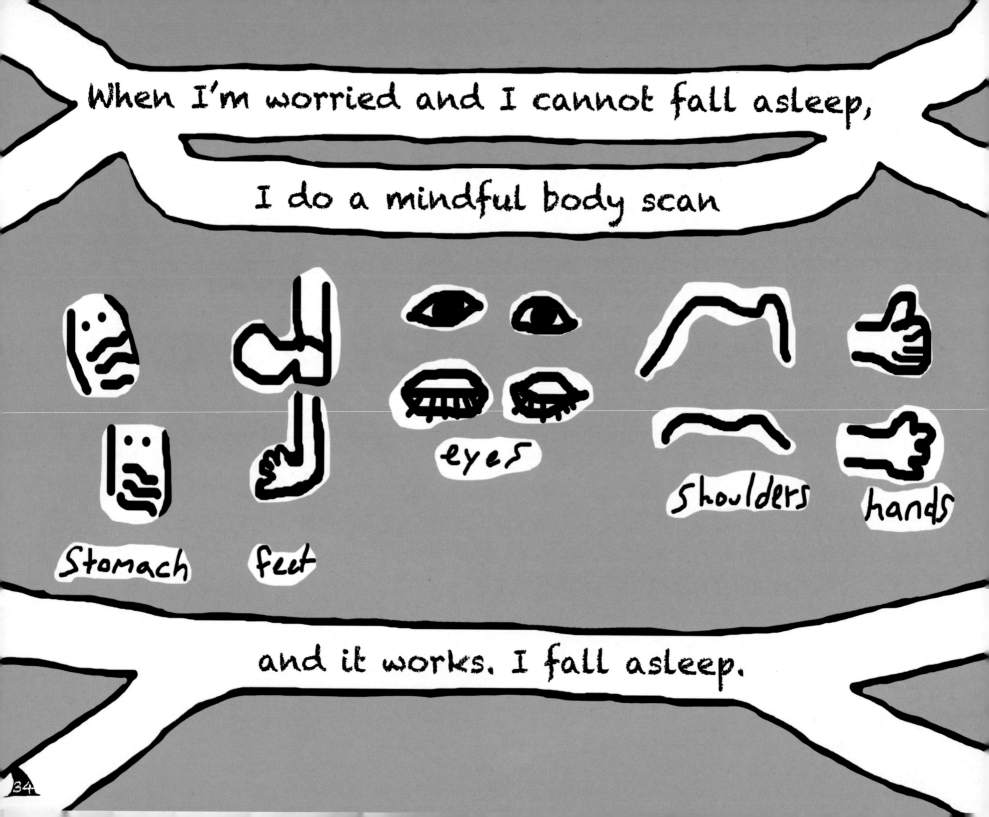

We use our bodies all the time, so it's important to pay attention to them. You can practice mindfulness by doing a body scan. You start by sitting in a chair or lying down. You pay attention to the feet for about 5 or 10 seconds, then move your attention to the toes for about 5 or 10 seconds, then move on to the ankles. You keep going body part by body part until you get to the head. You notice the different feelings or sensations your body is feeling. A sensation is a feeling like hot or cold, itchy, tingly, tight, painful or fine. Doing a body scan can make you feel better. It can help you feel your feelings and emotions and it can help you relax. When you can't sleep it's good to do a body scan because it can help you fall asleep.

What do we eat every day? Do you remember what you ate last night? Do you remember what it tasted like? Instead of being relaxed while we eat and paying attention to what we are eating, many times we are distracted by talking with our mouths full, watching tv, kicking each other under the table or texting while eating.

Sometimes we don't chew our food well. Often when we eat, we really don't know when we are hungry or full because we are not paying attention. To change this we are going to teach you to eat mindfully.

First, we observe our food. What color is it? How big is it? Does it look hard or soft? does it look like you

want to eat it or not? Can you imagine how it tastes? Then pay attention to the smell. Did it smell like you wanted it to smell? Now we're ready to taste the food. Take a little piece and put it on your tongue. Notice what happens. Now chew ten times before you swallow the food. You have just eaten mindfully! You can't eat everything like this but try and take a few mindful bites each day!

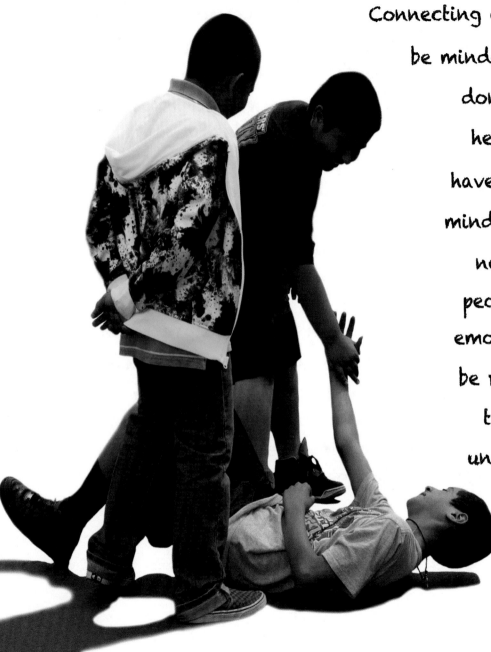

Connecting with other people is a way to be mindful. When people need help, don't make fun of them—try to help them. Everybody likes to have fun, but if you aren't being mindful, you won't have fun and neither will your friends. If people are upset or sad, angry, emotional or really happy, try to be respectful of their needs. Try to stand in their shoes and understand how they feel. Offer them help. Try to be kinder.

Sometimes you do mindfulness when you are still and sometimes you do mindfulness when you are moving.

Now we are going to teach you mindful walking.

To do mindful walking you have to focus on your feet. Try not to think of anything else. If your mind wanders away, just come back to your feet again.

Pick up one foot and move it forward and put your heel down and then put your toes down.

Pick up the other foot, move it forward and put your heel down and then put your toes down.

Keep repeating this for 15 steps. To turn around, you have to turn your body slowly until you are facing the other way. Pause. Then do it over again. Try to focus on your body, your legs, and your feet.

Mindful walking is important because it can help you calm down; it can make you feel safer. Also, if you practice mindful walking, you can move better whether you are walking, running or playing games or sports.

The following scripts will help guide you as you learn to practice mindfulness. Someone can read them to you or you could read and record them so you can listen to practice instructions in your own voice. We love mindfulness and we think you will too! The most important thing about mindfulness is remembering to do it.

There are four scripts here that will teach you the Sharkfin, Mindful Listening, Mindful Breathing, and the Body Scan.

We suggest you practice one lesson at a time. After you practice it a few times, you will probably find out that you don't need to listen to it anymore. You will just know it! However, listening to it will almost always help your focus stay in the practice.

So, let's get started with the Sharkfin!

Script 1   Getting Ready to Practice Mindfulness

-Doing the Sharkfin

To practice mindfulness you need to get ready and you get ready by doing the Sharkfin.

To do the Sharkfin, you put the side of your hand on your forehead with your thumb touching your forehead. Now move your hand down your face, in front of your nose. Say shhhh and close your eyes as your hand moves down. If you are sitting down, you do the 5 S's while you move your hand: Sit up straight, sit still, sit silently, soft breathing, and shut eyes. If you are standing you do the same but you are standing straight, still, silently, using soft breathing, and shut eyes while you move your hand down your face. You are now ready to practice mindfulness. (You can see a picture of one of us doing the sharkfin on page 6 in the book).

Script 2 Mindful Listening Instructions

Let's learn how to do mindful listening. First, do the sharkfin.

Please stay still and listen to the sound of the bell.

(Don't read this, just RING THE BELL and wait until the sound is gone before you read again.)

What did you hear?   (Pause, count to yourself to 5)
How did you feel? (Pause, count to yourself to 5)
What did you notice? (Pause, count to yourself to 5)

Now, please close your eyes and listen to the bell.

(Don't read this, just RING THE BELL and wait until the sound is gone before you read again.

How did it feel? (Pause, count to yourself to 5)

What were you thinking about? (Pause, count to yourself to 5)

Did you notice any difference between the 1st time and the 2nd time you heard the bell? (Pause, count to yourself to 5)

Many kids think it is easier to focus on your breath with your eyes closed.

Please do the Sharkfin. When you can't hear the bell anymore, please raise your hand. (Ring the bell.) How was it? (Pause, count to yourself to 5)

This time please listen to the sounds surrounding you. We'll do this for 30 seconds.

(Wait for 30 seconds.)

What did you hear? (Pause, count to yourself to 5) Were you surprised by the sounds you heard? (Pause, count to yourself to 5)

Congratulations! You've just learned mindful listening. Mindful listening will help you succeed through life.

Script 3 Mindful Breathing Instructions

Welcome to mindful breathing.

We're going to do three minutes of mindful breathing now but let's begin with the sharkfin to get ready.

Please put your hand with your thumb on top of your head. Slide your hand down the middle of your face, closing your eyes as soon as you get past your nose. Let's practice the 5 s's – Sit up straight, sit still, sit silently, shut eyes, and a soft breathing. That's what we call the Sharkfin. It's a shortcut for the 5 s's described above.

Now it's time for you to focus just on the breath.
Take a few breaths and see if you feel them in your nose, in your chest or in your belly.

(Pause for 10 counts.)

Pick the place to pay attention to your breath where you find your breath the easiest. If you can't tell where, pay attention to your belly going in and going out.

(Pause for 10 counts.)

Let's start with three deep breaths.

(DON'T READ THIS, Reader please take three breaths before continuing).

Breathing in & breathing out.

(TAKE ANOTHER THREE BREATHS).

Breathing in & breathing out.

(TAKE ANOTHER THREE BREATHS)
Soon you will notice that you have thoughts. Just notice them and let them pass. Return your focus to your breathing. This may happen several times. This is not a problem, it's just your brain at work. Your brain is always thinking, that's what brains do.

(45 SECONDS OF SILENCE)

Relaxing and focusing on your breath

(30 SECONDS OF SILENCE)

Breathing in & breathing out.

(30 SECONDS OF SILENCE)

Where is your mind now? Is it on your breath?

(15 SECONDS OF SILENCE)

We are going to ring the bell. When you can't hear the bell anymore, then open your eyes slowly and notice how you feel.

(RING BELL)

(WAIT TILL IT STOPS & THEN 5 SECONDS MORE)

It's good to practice mindful breathing every day. You can do it for as many minutes as you want, but try at least three. If you do mindfulness at the same time every day, it will be easier for you to remember to do it.

Script 4 Body Scan Instructions

One way to practice mindfulness is to do a body scan.

A body scan is when you pay attention to different parts of your body when they are still. You notice the different feelings or sensations your body is feeling. Doing a body scan can make you feel better. It can help you feel your feelings and emotions and it can help you relax. When you can't sleep it's good to do a body scan because it can help you fall asleep.

Let's do a body scan now. Please sit comfortably in a chair or on the floor or please lay down on the floor or on a bed. If you are in a chair please do the sharkfin because being alert will help you not fall asleep.

Please close your eyes.

Start by taking three deep breaths.
(TAKE THEM BEFORE YOU READ THE NEXT THING)

Then notice your feet. How do they feel? Are they cold, hot, tingly, tight or normal feeling? You might not feel anything and that's okay.

(COUNT TO 10 silently)

Now, move your awareness to your knees. How do they feel? Hard, soft, loose, weird, comfortable or painful?

(COUNT TO 10 silently)

Notice your legs. Do they feel loose or tight, tired or heavy from running too much? Can you feel your pants?

(COUNT TO 10 silently)

Now move your attention to your stomach. Does it feel full, empty, soft, hard, nervous or fine?

(COUNT TO 10 silently)

Move to your heart. Do you feel it beating? Does it hurt? Is it happy? Maybe you can't feel anything and that's okay.

Let's go to the back. Maybe it feels heavy or painful or tight or hot. Maybe it feels comfortable.

(COUNT TO 10 silently)

Let's move on to the shoulders. Do they feel hard, soft, tired or heavy? Or maybe they feel just fine. Just notice how they feel.

(COUNT TO 10 silently)

Pay attention to your arms. Do they feel hard, heavy, or light? Maybe you don't feel anything and that's okay.

(COUNT TO 10 silently)

Move on to the hands. What do you notice? Do they feel strong, soft, tired or nothing?

(COUNT TO 10 silently)

Then move to the fingers. Without moving the fingers, pay attention to how they feel. Do they feel tingly at your fingertips?

(COUNT TO 10 silently)

Now, let's go to the ears. You may hear noises or silence.

(COUNT TO 10 silently)

Let's pay attention to the eyes. Are they closed? If they are, are they closed loosely or tightly? Do they feel scratchy or burn? Do they feel fine?

(COUNT TO 10 silently)

Now let's move on to the top of the head, the holder of your amazing brain. Maybe you have a headache or maybe your head feels fine.

(COUNT TO 10 silently)

Please take three deep breaths again.

(COUNT TO 10 silently)

Let's head back down to your feet. Notice your shoulders, back, stomach, legs and feet.

(COUNT TO 10 silently)

(RING THE BELL...Wait till the sound is gone.)

Congratulations! You have just done a body scan!

Remember we said you could hear our voices leading you in mindfulness? Just go to http://www.newharbinger.com/34640 and ask an adult for help if you need it. We recorded instructions for Mindful Breathing, a body scan, Mindful Walking, Mindful Listening and Paying Attention Even When There are Distractions. We recommend you listen to them in a quiet place and don't listen to them in a car when someone is driving because it could make them relax too much and that could be dangerous.

Thanks for practicing mindfulness with us. We hope you enjoy it. We recommend that every day you practice some mindfulness. If you practice mindful breathing every day at the same time, it will be easier to remember to do it. Every night before sleeping you can do a body scan.

The more you practice mindfulness, the better you will get at finding your own superhero when you feel sad, angry, disappointed or any other strong emotion. You'll also enjoy your life more because you will be in the present moment and get to notice what is happening instead of planning or worrying so much.

Good luck, we wish you a happy life!

WE STRIVE TO BE MOMS – Masters of Mindfulness, 5th graders in Mr. Musumeci's class of 2013-2014 at Reach Academy in Oakland, California.

TRY IT! LOVE IT! DO IT!

"Peace. It does not mean to be in a place where there is no noise, trouble or hard work. It means to be in the midst of all those things and still be calm in your heart."

Unknown

Mason J. Musumeci has spent the last 20 years teaching, caring, and advocating for children from birth to school age in both New York City and California. Over the last 6 years he has worked with the students and families of Reach Academy in East Oakland to bring socially just and equitable education to the school as a 5th grade teacher, teacher leader, and currently in the role of Teacher on Special Assignment. Mason has been a proponent for Mindfulness within the school community for the last 3 years, after seeing its effect on both students and staff alike. The child of an Italian American family from Brooklyn, NY, Mason has realized the key role Mindfulness plays in supporting him to stay grounded in calmness during the moment to moment chaos of life.

Laurie Grossman, first and foremost is a social activist. She has spent the last 40 years looking for ways to make kids' lives better, particularly kids from vulnerable communities. Though Laurie believes that mindfulness is important for all students, regardless of their age or backgrounds, she knows from her career, what a very important tool mindfulness is for social justice and educational equity. For the last eight years her raison d'etre has been to spread mindfulness in schools as far and wide as possible. She helped found Mindful Schools at Park Day School in Oakland, California in 2007. Laurie is delighted to be the Director of Program Development and Outreach for Inner Explorer, a mindfulness in education non-profit. Her delight comes from the fact that she believes that Inner Explorer has discovered an easy and effective way to enable students and teachers to practice mindfulness daily in the classroom. Laurie lives in Oakland, Ca with her husband David Wright and a dog named Dallas. Ariel and Perrin, their kids, live in Boston and Portland. Laurie can be reached at lgrossman@innerexplorer.org.

In 2012 Angelina Alvarez was injured at work which led her to look for a pain management doctor. While dealing with chronic pain, mobility restrictions, insomnia, loss of family members, and panic attacks, Angelina was unable to photograph, an art practice that she pursued through graduation at the San Francisco Art Institute. With no outlet and in tremendous pain everyday, Angelina asked her doctor for options other than medication. Soon after, she was enrolled in an MBSR program that changed her life. At a point when being in her own skin no longer felt comfortable, Angelina was able to connect with her mind, body, and spirit. To her surprise she found her breath. Angelina left one MBSR session with balance and clarity understanding that every child should have the opportunity to grow up with the foundation of a mindfulness practice. Angelina teaches mindfulness with Mindful Life Project in her hometown of Richmond, California, and enjoys it moment by moment.

Mr. Musumeci's 5th Grade Class 2013-2014

Jessica Arellano
Tamarion Batson
Natalie Benavides
Isaac Camacho
Carlos Castañeda
Terrea Curry
Yeira Torres Felix
Akejsia Hardaway
Keyon Johnson
Jazmine Jones
Angel Hernandez
Viridiana Hernandez Arenal
Osirys Marquez-Manzo
Jefferson Melendez
Sir-Jantz Moliga
Fatima Morales
Queenilyah Prejean
Eric Reyes
Jose Ramirez
Bryant Rojas
Kevin Romero
Blaire Swan
Alexis Gameliel Velazquez
Rodrick Watson
Samearra Watts
Harris Cox, Mindfulness Teacher

Acknowledgments

My parents, Ivan and Sherry Grossman, and my grandma, Rose Feinstein, always inspired me to work to make this world a better place. Though they are no longer alive, I think this book would make them happy. In my 40 years of trying to make the world more equitable for children, mindfulness is the tool that I have found most effective in helping children help themselves. This book is actually a demonstration of this finding. I am grateful to the children who wrote this book but also to so many people, without whom this book would not exist.

I would like to thank Tom Little and Park Day School for encouraging our experiment to bring mindfulness to children in Oakland, California, in 2007. I appreciate Alba Witkin, The Wayne & Gladys Valley Foundation, The Fleishhacker, Y & H Soda, & WHH Foundations, a variety of Haas Foundations, and Peter Wilson and Mary Ann Cobb for supporting Park's Community Outreach Program for over a decade, laying the groundwork for public schools to be receptive to that experiment. Thanks to Richard Shankman, a wonderful mindfulness teacher, and Diana Winston for sharing curriculum enabling us to launch a pilot program which became an immediate success at Emerson Elementary School in North Oakland. Shortly thereafter, Megan Cowan joined us and brought important insights into crafting and improving our curriculum. I appreciate Richard, Megan, Kate Janke and all the other mindfulness teachers who taught me so much and helped create a vibrant organization called Mindful Schools. I appreciate Randy Fernando for understanding and promoting the importance of this work through Mindful Schools.

I will always be indebted to one of my most important mindfulness teachers, Jon Kabat-Zinn. His enthusiasm for our work in the early days was inspiring. When he found out I didn't have a mindfulness practice, he immediately sent me CD's to get me practicing. Now, almost eight years later, I am very grateful to him for his help in launching my practice and for recognizing the importance of this book by writing the foreword. Gina Biegel, author of *The Stress Reduction Workbook for Teens: Mindfulness Skills to Help You Deal with Stress*, was another important mentor from the beginning. She was instrumental in helping me understand the value of this work, and in helping to advance the movement to bring mindfulness to youth. Linda Graham, author of *Bouncing Back, Rewiring Your Brain for Maximum Resilience* and *Well-Being,* has been an important source of wisdom, support, and inspiration for me. I am heartfully grateful to Laura Bakosh and Janice Houlihan of Inner Explorer for devising a wonderful system to create daily practice in schools. It is a privilege to have been invited to join their team.

Thank you to Isaac Camacho, a fifth grader in Mr. Musumeci's class, who came up with the idea for our book, Master of Mindfulness. Mr. Musumeci was wonderfully supportive and allowed us to work with his class several times a week, for several months, to produce their ideas, writing and artwork. To Mr. Musumeci's entire fifth-grade class of 2013-2014, thank you for your spunk, playfulness, enthusiasm about mindfulness, hard work, and desire to share mindfulness with other kids. I am incredibly grateful to our book designer, Angelina Alvarez. I had no idea how we were going to pull together and organize the students' work into a book. In walked Angelina, artistic, brilliant, talented, and an amazing mindfulness teacher. My childhood friend of longest standing, Lori Sadewitz, was immensely helpful in editing, reading, and rereading to get the book where it is today. Thanks also go to Stacey Daraio for teaching me the Sharkfin.

I am so grateful to David Wright, my amazing husband, for encouraging me to pursue this work, for giving advice, for editing, for taking that first MBSR class with me, and for listening to years of my exciting daily tales about mindfulness in schools. I am head-over-heels grateful for our own children, Ariel and Perrin, who "shared me" with the thousands of kids who were learning mindfulness. My sisters Jane Grossman, Nancy Grossman-Samual, Dina Kjaergaard, and Betty Herring have been stalwart supporters and continue to send me important information about mindfulness almost weekly. Finally, thanks go to Bertha Reilly, Steve Brown, Harris Cox, Tracey Edwards, Elizabeth Little, Angela Haick, Jackie Krentzman, Janette Hernandez, Neela Manley, Cassandra McCraw, Lara Mendel, Sam Piha, Brad Rassler, Bob Stahl, Pam Nicholls, Marjie Chaset, Mary Reilly, Betsy Rose, and Sue Schleifer, who have all been instrumental in supporting me through this journey.

My hope is that this book will help spread mindfulness by enabling kids, parents, and educators to understand this valuable and essential life skill.

Laurie Grossman

To all the kiddos, allow the breath to keep you connected to yourself. Mindfully listen to your heart and if there is anything that makes you sad or hurts you, use your words to explain how your heart feels. If you are scared to speak, take a deep breath and speak. Your voice is who you are inside. With every exhale love yourself. Imagine your strength when you have your friends' back; now give the same strength to yourself, the words, the stern face, the backup. Have that for your own heart and speak your words. The breath will guide you. Much love and gratitude to my mother Joanne; thank you for believing me. Mom, Aunt Lorraine, Aunt Ceci, Uncle Randy thank you for giving me the strength and backbone I have today. Thank you to Dr. Hebrard and Tobi Allen for helping me start the process of rewiring my brain for resilience.

To the fifth graders, amazing job! I had fun working with you all! Keep the creativity going and shine! Light!

Angelina Alvarez

Mindfulness is a seed growing inside your body. The best way to help the seed grow faster is to practice mindfulness. You water the seed of mindfulness when you do the Sharkfin and when you say, " I have the power to make wise choices." You water it when you do mindful breathing, mindful walking or a body scan. The more you practice, the easier it is to call on your superhero when you need him or her.

"Given the landscape of today's teen's mental and physical health difficulties, the earlier you can plant the seeds of mindfulness the stronger the roots become and the sprouts more prodigious. After working with thousands of teens in education and therapy, I believe that if they had been offered these skills earlier they would have fared better and had stronger roots for which to approach and manage the landscape of today's adolescent. *Master of Mindfulness* gets it! It gets that these skills know no age boundaries, class boundaries or race boundaries. Mindfulness helps children to fare well in this growing, fast-paced and technologically stimulated lifescape that we call the 21st century. Bravo Grossman, Alvarez, Musumeci & most prominently the 5th grade children!"

Gina M. Biegel, MA, LMFT, researcher, author of *The Stress Reduction Workbook for Teens*, founder of the Mindfulness-Based Stress Reduction Program for Teens (MBSR-T) & Stressed Teens Program

"Safety is an embodied place inside our bodies. Learning to experience safety is the first step in healing the behavioral and emotional effects of trauma and profoundly overwhelming life experiences. If we want to teach kids how to take charge of their lives, how to make wise choices, how to be empowered to realize their dreams, we first need to teach them how to feel safe. The transformative practice that the teachers and students describe in *Master of Mindfulness, Finding your own Superhero in Times of Stress* is the cornerstone of building an internal safe place. Give a copy of this book to every kid you know!"

Marjie Chaset, LMFT

"*Master of Mindfulness* brings such joy to the reader – students, teachers, parents – by showing us the power of mindfulness to help young people cope with their own thoughts, their peers, their world, more resiliently, more authentically, more creatively. These mindfulness-based tools mature students' capacities to skillfully navigate their increasingly complex world as adults. A true gift."

Linda Graham, MFT, psychotherapist, author of *Bouncing Back: Rewiring Your Brain for Maximum Resilience and Well-Being*